Healthy

Margaret Flynn,
illustrated Catherine Brighton

Gaskell/St George's Hospital Medical School
LONDON

This is the story our advisors Paul, Anya, Geraldine, Nigel and Peter saw in the pictures.

1.   Joe is wrapping birthday presents.

2.   It's Lynne's birthday. Lynne opens her cards and presents at breakfast.

3.   Her presents are for the kitchen.

4.   Matt and Lynne look at one of her presents. It's a cook book from Joe.

5.   They watch a cooking programme on TV. The programme shows how to cut a lemon.

6.   Lynne rings Joe on her mobile phone.

7a. Joe comes to visit.

7   They are getting ready for a party.

8.   Lynne thanks Joe for her presents. Matt and Lynne show Joe what they want to cook.

9a. They all go out together.

9.   Joe helps Matt and Lynne choose some food to cook. First they choose some chicken.

10. Now they choose some party food. They put crisps and fizzy drinks in the trolley.

11. Next they choose some fruit and vegetables.

12. Matt and Lynne pay for the food at the checkout.

13a. The shopping is heavy. They all carry some.

13. Everything goes in the fridge. The food keeps fresh in the fridge.

14. They all wash their hands. Lynne ties her apron.

15. Joe shows them how to cut up the meat and vegetables. They use one chopping board for the meat and one for the vegetables. The cookbook is open at the right page.

16. Something is steaming.

17. Joe holds the saucepan handle carefully. He stirs the food.

18. Matt puts the crisps into a bowl.

19. Joe sees a small toy in the bowl of crisps. It was in the packet. He takes it out so that no one will swallow it.

20. Now Joe brings in the food.

21. People arrive at the party. Some friends give Lynne a present.

22. Joe passes the food around.

23. There are lots of people. They enjoy the food and have a good time.

24. Some people are dancing. Nobody talks to Karen. She feels lonely. She eats more cake to comfort herself.

25. Jon tips a packet of nuts into his mouth.

26. Oh no! Jon chokes on the nuts.

27. Carol pats him on the back. She is worried about Jon. Jon coughs up the nuts.

28. He sits down to recover and drinks a glass of water.

29. Most people are having fun. No one talks to Karen. She's eating more cake.

30. Karen sleeps in a chair. Other people clear up.

31. The party ends. Matt and Lynne wave goodbye.

32. Matt and Lynne go shopping again.

33. They meet Karen in the street.

34. Matt invites Karen to come home with them.

35. Karen helps to unload the shopping.

36. They all wash their hands. Matt puts on an apron.

37. They prepare the food and start to cook.

38. Now they wait for the food to cook.

39. Lynne, Matt and Karen enjoy eating the food. They are happy.

40. Lynne puts some grapes in a bag. They are for Karen.

41. Karen takes the grapes. She says goodbye and goes home.

42. Lynne and Matt relax together.

Enjoying healthy eating

This book is about food for ourselves, for our families and for our friends. It is about enjoying different kinds of food. It is about taking time to get food ready for eating, making sure that it looks nice and smells so good you want to eat it. It is about food that tastes good and can be eaten safely.

Eating is important for all of us. Different kinds of food give our bodies energy. How much energy our bodies need depends on:

- How old we are (older people need less energy than younger people),

- Whether we are men or women (women need less energy than men).

- How heavy we are. Heavier people need more energy to do the same amount of work as people who are not heavy.

- The kinds of lives we have and how much exercise we do.

- Whether we are sick or not well, e.g. while a raised temperature may increase our energy needs, mostly people who are sick need less energy.

- People who need a lot of help to move and walk may be using less energy.

It is important that we:

- Drink plenty of water every day.

- Move and keep fit by walking (or dancing, jogging, cycling, swimming, or going to the gym) because exercise keeps our bones and muscles strong.

- Get the balance right between what we eat and what our bodies need.

- Drink sensibly, if we drink alcohol.

'Five-a-day' and more

In this book, Lynne and Matt ask a friend to help them to cook. They learn lots of important things. They learn about:

- Planning what kind of food to buy.

- Making sure that the food they buy and cook is fresh.

- Eating five portions of fruit and vegetables every day.

- Washing their hands before getting food ready to eat.

- Having a clean kitchen with clean worktops and clean knives, forks and spoons.

- Eating food that is good for our bodies: eating more foods that grow from plants, like fruit, vegetables, beans, nuts and lentils.

Matt and Lynne know that they should be eating more fruit and vegetables. Most of us aren't eating enough.

We should encourage each other to eat healthily and take exercise. Our bodies are designed to be active. The more active we are, the more energy we have. Yet many of us spend too much time indoors watching TV and snacking, even though we may not be hungry. Eating healthily means eating a wide range of foods. Eating different kinds of foods may seem more expensive, but it is really worth doing for the sake of our health.

What food to eat every day

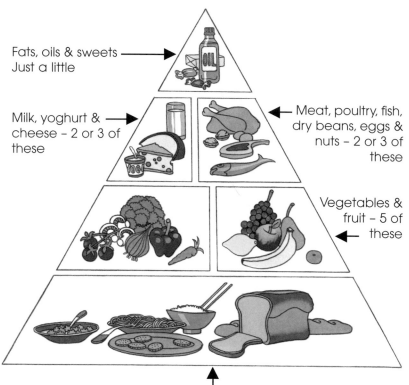

Fats, oils & sweets
Just a little

Milk, yoghurt &
cheese – 2 or 3 of
these

Meat, poultry, fish,
dry beans, eggs &
nuts – 2 or 3 of
these

Vegetables &
fruit – 5 of
these

Bread, cereal, rice & pasta – 5 of these

This picture shows the recommended balance of foods
that we should eat. It aims to help us understand and
enjoy healthy eating. It shows how people don't have
to give up the food they most enjoy for the sake of their
health. Just eat some in smaller amounts and less often.

When we're trying to make a healthy choice, for most of
us the aim should be to **eat more** fruit and vegetables

Fruit and vegetables should make up one third of the food we eat. We should aim to eat at least five portions every day. These can be tinned, frozen, dried, cooked or raw. A glass of fruit juice can also make up one portion each day. A portion means one apple or banana, or two smaller fruits such as plums, or two to three tablespoons of frozen vegetables. It's best to vary the types of fruit and vegetables you eat.

Starchy foods should also make up about one third of our diet. These include bread, breakfast cereals, pasta, rice, potatoes, beans and lentils. We should try to eat a variety of these foods and choose wholegrain, wholemeal or 'high fibre' varieties wherever possible.

Some people think that starchy foods are fattening. This isn't true. It's the margarine or butter we spread on bread and the cream or cheese sauce we add to pasta, or the oil we use for frying that makes starchy foods fattening.

A healthy diet means eating and drinking less fat and sugar. Everyone probably eats some foods containing fat every day, such as margarine or butter, cooking oils, oil-based salad dressings and mayonnaise. Keep these to small amounts and choose low-fat varieties.

Protein

For most people, a balanced diet will include some, but not too much, protein every day. The following foods contain protein: meat and poultry, fish, eggs, milk, cheese, tofu, nuts and pulses such as peas, lentils and beans.

Fibre

Fibre – what we used to call roughage – does more than prevent constipation. Lack of fibre can cause other bowel problems and may contribute to diabetes and heart disease. These foods contain lots of fibre: fruit, vegetables, potatoes (with the skin on), bread, bran in cereals and baked beans.

Salt

Some recent reports suggest that eating too much salt can lead to high blood pressure. And high blood pressure increases the risk of stroke and heart disease. So, it's important to avoid eating a lot of food with high levels of salt. Eating a balanced diet with a wide range of different kinds of foods can help us to achieve this aim. Looking at food labels helps us to choose which foods are best for us. Although most of the salt we eat in our diet comes from processed foods, we should also consider adding less during cooking and at the table.

Fat

Some fat in the diet is important for health. But eating too much is linked to becoming overweight. Looking at food labels can help you choose which foods you need. Some types of fat can increase the risk of heart disease. These are found in meat and dairy products such as meat pies, cheese, sausages, butter, biscuits and cakes. But some types of fat are essential in small amounts in the diet. These include vegetable oils and oily fish such as salmon, mackerel, sardines, pilchards or herrings.

We should aim to eat at least two portions of fish each week, one of which should be an oily fish.

Sugar

We don't need to add sugar to our diet as the body gets what it requires from the foods we eat. So, it's important to avoid eating a lot of food with high levels of sugar. Eating a balanced diet with a wide range of different kinds of food can help us to achieve this aim. Looking at food labels helps us to choose which foods are best for us. Although most of the sugar we eat in our diet comes from processed foods, we should also consider adding less during cooking and at the table.

Special diets

Diabetes – People with diabetes have too much sugar in their blood. This can make them feel grumpy, tired or dizzy. It can also make them very thirsty. They need to eat a healthy diet without much sugar. They may have to take medicine every day. They must eat their meals at regular times and take lots of exercise.

Being overweight – Healthy eating and taking more exercise is the best way to lose weight. This can make us feel better and improve our health. Eat three meals a day and try not to snack between meals. Eat lots of fruit, vegetables and starchy foods such as bread, cereal and potatoes. Our doctor can refer us to a dietician for special advice.

Being underweight – Some people do not eat enough to maintain a healthy body weight. There can be many different reasons for this. For example, someone might be a very slow and fussy eater and, in a group-living situation, simply not have time to eat enough food to meet their energy requirements. Some people have a poor appetite – this might be connected with illness such as depression, an infection or toothache. If someone continues to lose weight, it is important to get medical advice because it can mean the person is ill.

Eating Disorders – Some people are overweight or underweight because of an eating disorder. If you think someone may have an eating disorder, suggest they ask their doctor for advice.

Gluten-free and casein-free diets – Wheat, rye, barley and oats all contain gluten. People who have coeliac disease cannot eat food containing any gluten at all. Some people cannot eat anything with wheat or milk in it. Their doctor or dietician will advise if they should take any vitamin or mineral food supplements. This is because they may be missing some of the goodness in bread, milk and cereals if they are on a gluten-, wheat- or dairy-free diet.

Choking

Some people are more likely to choke than others. They include people who need a lot of assistance because of their physical disabilities; people with a history of breathing problems; and people who take tranquillisers (or medicine for their mood or behaviour). It also includes people with Down's syndrome. Some people 'bolt' their food or take food from other people's plates. This is sometimes seen in people who have moved out of long-stay institutions, where they may not have had enough food to eat. Some people do not chew their food properly – this may be because they have problems with their teeth.

Choking is more common with dry, crumbly food such as biscuits, crisps and nuts. It can happen if food is tipped directly from a packet into the mouth. It can also happen if other items are put in the mouth, such as plastic toys found in cereal packets and in other snacks, such as crisps. It is important that people who are at greater risk of choking are watched as they eat or are fed.

People who are worried about choking can ask for a choking risk assessment. Speech and language therapists can do these assessments.

Sometimes when people choke, they can get a chest infection later. It is important that a doctor treats chest infections properly. This is because more people die from 'aspiration pneumonia' (which is a chest infection caused by something 'going down the wrong way'), than from the choking itself.

Ideas for service providers

Supporters and residential, day and leisure staff have a duty of care to the people they support. Sometimes supporters are unsure about whether it is all right for someone to eat whatever they want. But their duty of care includes supporting people by helping them to understand how to keep healthy. Here are some ideas.

- Offer a choice of pudding, e.g. fruit **or** cake, or only offer cake once or twice a week.

- If someone has a poor diet, e.g. is eating a poor variety of foods, ask a dietician for advice on improving intake.

- At a cookery session, teach how to make healthier food items containing more fruit and vegetables.

- Ask doctors and pharmacists about the medication people are taking, e.g. is it linked with weight gain?

- Make exercising three times a week a high priority. Can people go swimming or for a walk in the park? Can they walk to their day centres and clubs instead of being collected by bus?

- Offer a choice of healthy food options at parties and social clubs, e.g. fruit, vegetables with dips, water and diet drinks or fruit juice.

- Remember that *your* eating habits may influence the person you are supporting.

- Help people to choose food wisely if you eat out, e.g. eat a wide range of foods but less deep-fried food and less food with sauces.

- Encourage people to drink lots of water.

You can photocopy these Do's and Don'ts to fit particular advice to individuals.

Don't   **Do**

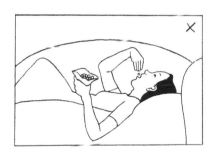 

Don't　　　　**Do**

 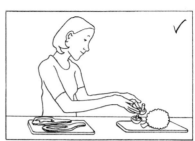

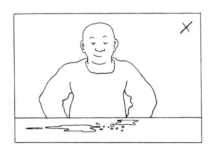 

Don't   **Do**

Where to find help and advice

For advice about healthy eating and diets, contact your doctor, who may wish to refer you to a dietician.

Community Teams for People with Learning Disabilities (CTPLDs). These are specialist multi-disciplinary health and social care teams that support adults with learning disabilities and their families. Some teams include a speech and language therapist or will be able to refer you to a dietician. Your doctor or social services department should have the address of the local CTPLD.

Some Further Education Colleges provide cookery classes for people with learning disabilities. It is worth checking if your local college provides such courses.

Written information

Choking Risks for Adults with Learning Disabilities. Of 674 carers of adults with learning disabilities who completed a questionnaire survey about the person's experience of choking, 27 were interviewed in more depth because of a serious episode of choking. The study found out that the risk of choking was greater if someone was taking more than one 'psychotropic' medicine. It was also greater if they had no teeth or had teeth in poor condition. This report is available at a small charge from the Department of Psychiatry of Disability, St George's Hospital Medical School, Jenner Wing, Cranmer Terrace, London SW17 0RE. Tel: 020 8725 5496; Fax: 020 8672 1070.

Advice on healthy eating can also be found on the website of the Food Standards Agency at www.foodstandards.gov.uk/healthiereating/

The Balance of Good Health: Information for Educators and Communicators. This is a pictorial representation of the recommended balance of foods in the diet that aims to help you understand and enjoy healthy eating. Available free from the Food Standards Agency.

The Food Standards Agency produces many free leaflets about healthy eating and related subjects. For a publications list and copies of the leaflets, telephone 0845 606 0667; Minicom: 0845 606 0678; Fax: 020 8867 3225 or e-mail: foodstandards@ecologistics.co.uk

Catering Guide to the Gluten Free Diet. A free leaflet is available to people with coeliac disease from Coeliac UK, Publications Department, PO Box 220, High Wycombe, Buckinghamshire HP11 2HY. Helpline: 0870 444 8804; Tel: 01494 437278.

What to do when you have Type 1 diabetes? and *What to do when you have Type 2 diabetes?* These two leaflets are produced by Diabetes UK with help from CHANGE, a national organisation run by and for people with learning disabilities. They are available free of charge from Diabetes UK, 10 Parkway, London NW1 7AA. Tel: 020 7424 1000; Fax: 020 7424 1001; e-mail: info@diabetes.org.uk

Other titles in the Books Beyond Words series

Using health services is explained in *Going to the Doctor, Going to Out-Patients* and *Going into Hospital. Looking After My Breasts* and *Keeping Healthy 'Down Below'* are about breast and cervical screening. *Getting on with Cancer* deals honestly with the unpleasant side of treatment but ends on a positive note.

Mugged tells what happens to a young man after he is attacked and robbed in the street.

Three books cover access to criminal justice as a victim (witness) or as a defendant: *Going to Court, You're Under Arrest* and *You're on Trial.*

Speaking Up For Myself shows how people with learning disabilities who come from ethnic minority groups have the right to challenge discrimination.

The difficult subject of sexual abuse is covered in *Bob Tells All, Jenny Speaks Out* and *I Can Get Through It.* The third title explains about counselling and psychotherapy after sexual abuse.

Forming new relationships is the subject of *Making Friends* and *Hug Me, Touch Me.* The ups and downs of a romantic relationship are traced in *Falling in Love.*

Two books about personal care are *George Gets Smart* and *Susan's Growing Up.* The latter tells the story of a young girl's first menstruation.

Michelle Finds a Voice explains methods of augmentative communication.

Peter's New Home and *A New Home in the Community* help explain about moving home.

To order copies (at £10.00 each; £9.00 each for 10 or more books) or for a leaflet giving more information, please contact: Book Sales, Royal College of Psychiatrists, 17 Belgrave Square, London SW1X 8PG. Credit card orders can be taken by telephone (020 7235 2351, extension 146).